THE KINGDOMS AND EMPIRES OF ANCIENT AFRICA

HISTORY OF THE ANCIENT WORLD

Children's History Books

BABY PROFESSOR
EDUCATION KIDS

Speedy Publishing LLC

40 E. Main St. #1156

Newark, DE 19711

www.speedypublishing.com

Copyright 2017

In this book, we're going to talk about the kingdoms and empires of ancient Africa. So, let's get right to it!

The first human civilization was in Africa, so Africa has had a long history with the rise and collapse of many different empires and kingdoms. The civilization of the ancient Egyptians lasted over 3,000 years, but they weren't the only great civilizations that developed in Africa.

Some of the major civilizations, including Ancient Egypt, were:

- Ancient Egypt, in the northeast section of Africa
- The Kingdom of Ghana, in the western section of Africa
- The Mali Empire, in the western section of Africa

- The Songhai Empire, in the western section of Africa
- The Kingdom of Kush, in the northeast section of Africa

KINGDOM OF KUSH RUINS

- The Kingdom of Aksum, in the eastern section of Africa
- The Central African Kingdoms, in the vast regions of central Africa

ANCIENT EGYPT

ANCIENT EGYPT

The civilization of ancient Egypt lasted from 3150 BC to 30 BC. The Nile River was the source of the Egyptians' prosperity. From the very beginning, they used the water and fertile soil that was brought by the river to farm.

They developed advanced techniques including saving water for irrigation during times when the river wasn't providing enough. They also invented ways to determine when the river was going to flood. In fact, they became so expert at farming that they were able to provide enough for their own people to eat, but also had excess to sell.

ANCIENT EGYPT WATER SYSTEM

Historians divide the timeline of Egypt into three major periods with periods in between described as intermediate periods. During the major periods, the civilization was strongest. The three major periods were the Old, Middle, and New Kingdoms.

B ecause of their strength in farming, the ancient Egyptians were able to diversify and take on other roles. Some people worked in the government and reported to the leader of the civilization who was called the Pharaoh.

PHARAOH

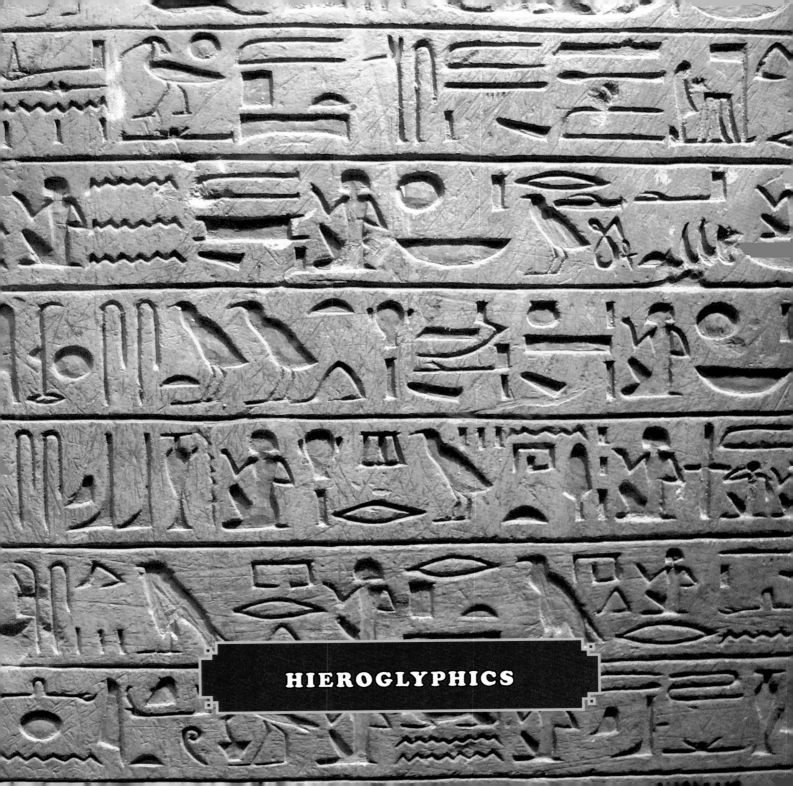

HIEROGLYPHICS

There were priests who tended to the temples of the many gods they worshipped as well as scholars and scribes who wrote the ancient language of hieroglyphics. There were also thousands of workers who built the massive pyramids and temples, some of which are still standing today after thousands of years.

THE KINGDOM OF GHANA

The kingdom of Ghana, which existed from 300 AD to 1100 AD, was situated in the western portion of Africa, south of the expansive Sahara desert. Today, that same area is divided into the country of Mauritania as well as the country of Senegal and modern-day Mali. The area was primarily grasslands, called the savanna, and there were some major rivers running through it, including the Gambia, Senegal, and Niger rivers.

Hut village in Ghana

The kingdom was founded when the Soninke population united their many tribes under their first ruler, who was called Dinga Cisse. The government was structured as a feudal system. This simply means that there were local rulers who were in charge of their own lands, but they paid tribute to the king.

Bareina, a village in southwestern Mauritania

Caravan

Iron and gold mines were the resources that brought them prosperity. They established trade routes and carried these exports across the Sahara desert using camel caravans. They exchanged their goods with the northern African Muslims to obtain cloth, work tools, farm livestock, and salt, which was considered to be just as valuable as gold.

THE MALI EMPIRE

Eventually the empire of Ghana collapsed and became part of the empire of Mali. The empire of Mali became very large over time. Its border to the north was at the southern edge of the Sahara desert. The kingdom covered a width of 1,200 miles from the interior trading city of Gao to Africa's west coast facing the Atlantic ocean. Today the area it encompassed has been divided into six countries.

MALI WARLORDS

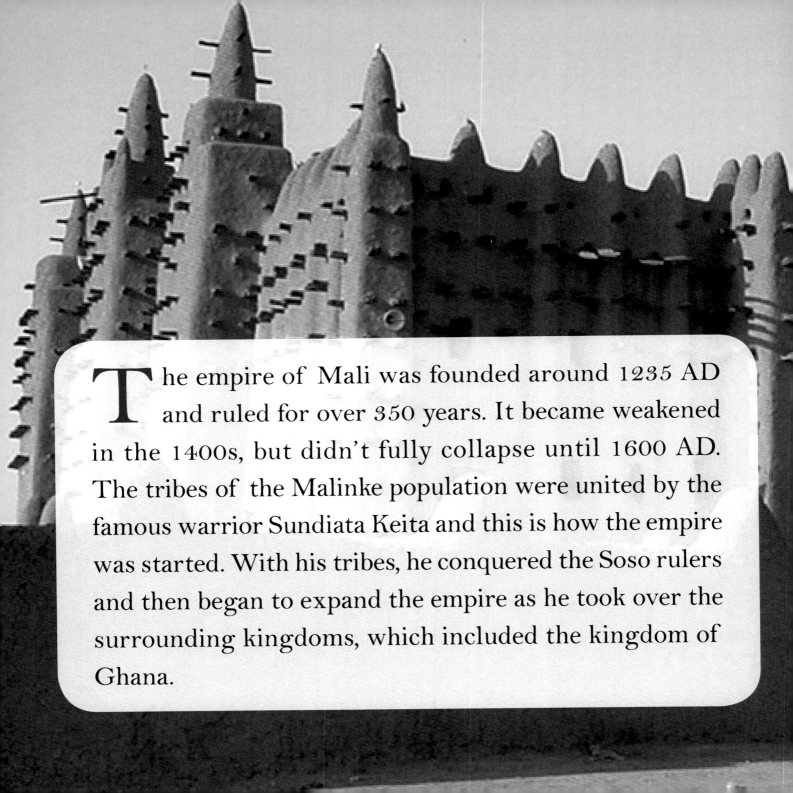

The empire of Mali was founded around 1235 AD and ruled for over 350 years. It became weakened in the 1400s, but didn't fully collapse until 1600 AD. The tribes of the Malinke population were united by the famous warrior Sundiata Keita and this is how the empire was started. With his tribes, he conquered the Soso rulers and then began to expand the empire as he took over the surrounding kingdoms, which included the kingdom of Ghana.

MUD MOSQUE, MALI

The kings of the Mali Empire were called Mansas. They governed the entire kingdom but the region of land was so vast that it was divided into sections called provinces. Each province was ruled by a government official called a ferba.

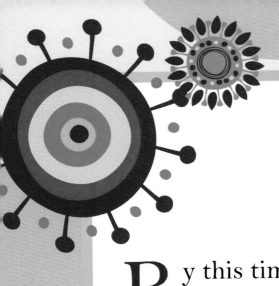

By this time, the religion of Islam had come to Africa and many of the rulers in the Mali governments were Muslims. The rulers were tolerant of the native African religions so the people didn't have to convert to Islam if they didn't wish to. Many Mali people practiced a religion that incorporated some of the beliefs of Islam into their traditional African rituals.

Mosque in Mali

GAO, NIGER RIVER

THE SONGHAI EMPIRE

Before the 1400s, the Songhai people were ruled by the leaders of the empire of Mali. A Songhai prince by the name of Sunni Ali was thrown in prison by the Mali leaders due to his political views. He managed to escape and he fled to the capital city of Gao.

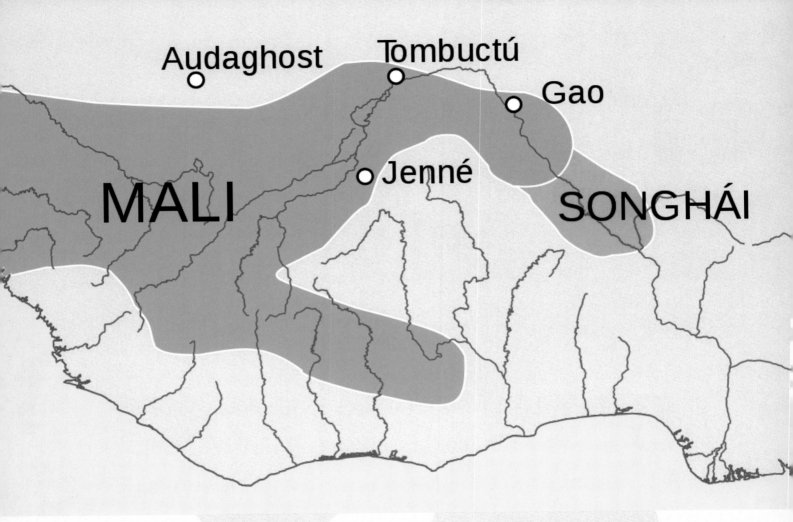

Audaghost   Tombuctú

Gao

MALI   Jenné   SONGHÁI

With his followers, he overthrew the government there. From that base, he founded the Songhai Empire in 1464 AD. The Songhai Empire stayed in power in Western Africa for over 125 years.

S unni Ali began to conquer the neighboring regions and he eventually took over the important trade city of Timbuktu as well as the city of Djenne.

CITY OF DJENNE TODAY

SALT

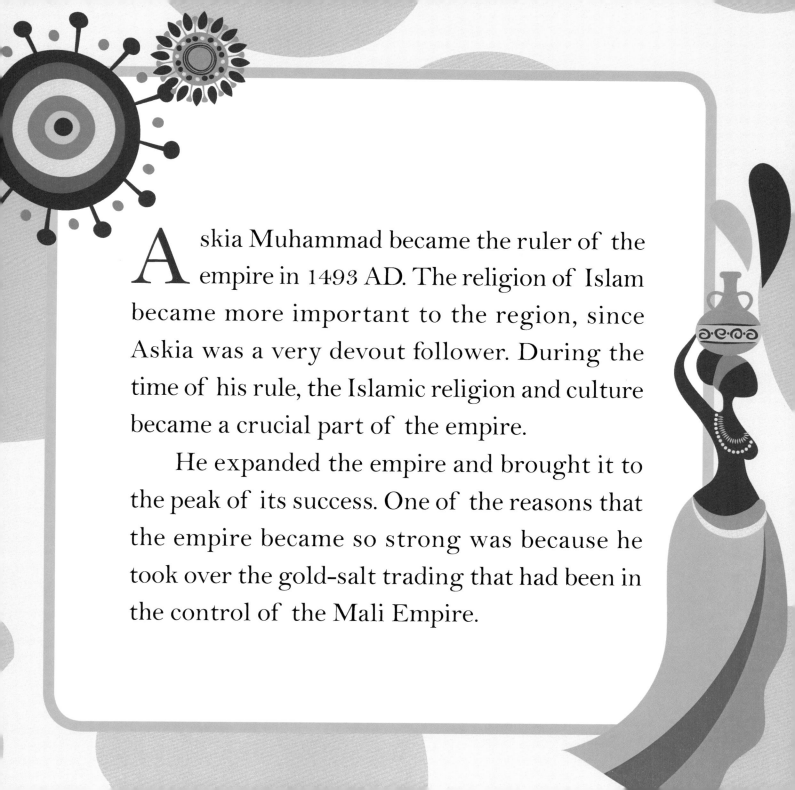

Askia Muhammad became the ruler of the empire in 1493 AD. The religion of Islam became more important to the region, since Askia was a very devout follower. During the time of his rule, the Islamic religion and culture became a crucial part of the empire.

He expanded the empire and brought it to the peak of its success. One of the reasons that the empire became so strong was because he took over the gold-salt trading that had been in the control of the Mali Empire.

The trading of slaves became an important part of the empire's economy. Slaves were needed to carry exports across the Sahara to the trading ports of Morocco as well as the Middle East. When the Muslim rulers captured nearby areas, they took prisoners of war and enslaved them. Many of these slaves were sold to families in Europe as well as in the Americas.

CARAVAN IN SAHARA

NUBIA, PIRAMIDI
KHARTOUM

THE KINGDOM OF KUSH

The Kingdom of Kush, also known as Nubia, became independent from ancient Egypt around 1070 BC. The region was at the intersection of the White Nile and the Blue Nile rivers. Today, the modern-day country of Sudan is situated at the site. The kingdom reigned for more than 1400 years.

ASSYRIAN WAR CHARIOT

The rulers became very powerful and they took control of the civilization of Egypt in 727 BC and reigned until the Assyrians overthrew Egypt. The city of Napata was the capital during the empire's peak.

However, as battling with their former country intensified, the government of Kush moved the capital to the city of Meroe, which was further south, away from the borderline fighting.

Pyramids of Kush

The government and people of Kush retained their Egyptian heritage in many ways. Their government, religion, and culture were all based on Egyptian traditions. They even built pyramids like the Egyptians. The people were masters at archery and the lands were nicknamed "Land of the Bow."

THE KINGDOM OF AKSUM

The Aksum Kingdom was located on the east coast of Africa on the western side of the Red Sea. The Red Sea separates the African continent from the Arabian Peninsula and during a portion of its reign, it also had territories that were east of the Red Sea. It's believed that the kingdom was founded around 400 BC by the son of King Solomon of Israel and the mysterious Queen of Sheba. The empire began to gain power around 100 AD and then reached its peak during the rule of King Ezana, who was leader from 325 AD through 360 AD.

Ezana had converted to Christianity so the Christian religion became the main religion. During his rule, he overthrew the Kingdom of Kush and took over its capital city, Meroe.

THE CENTRAL AFRICAN KINGDOMS

There were six major civilizations that occupied Central Africa during ancient times.

- The Sao Civilization
- The Kingdom of Zimbabwe
- The Kongo Kingdom
- The Luba Kingdom
- The Lunda Kingdom
- The Mutapa Kingdom

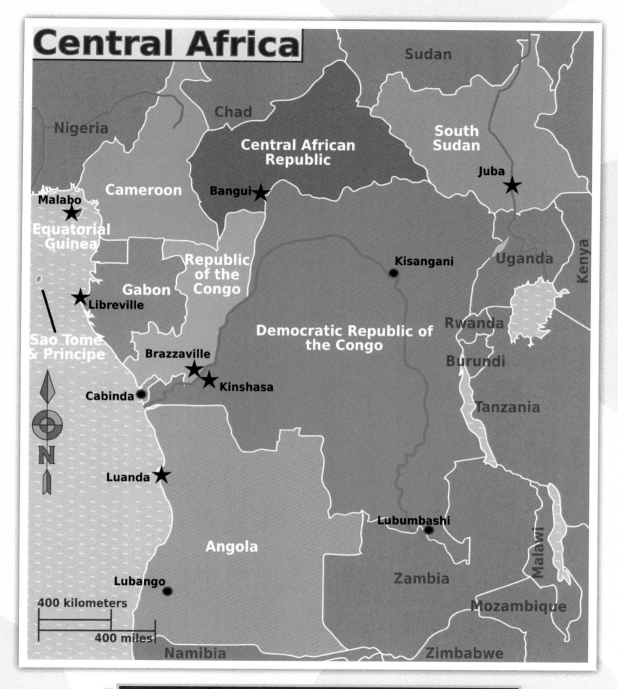

Central Africa

Sudan

Nigeria

Chad

Central African Republic

South Sudan

Juba ★

Cameroon

Bangui ●★

Malabo ★

Equatorial Guinea

Republic of the Congo

Kisangani ●

Uganda

Gabon

Libreville ★

Sao Tome & Principe

Democratic Republic of the Congo

Rwanda

Burundi

Brazzaville ★

Kinshasa ●★

Cabinda ●

Tanzania

N

Luanda ★

Lubumbashi ●

Angola

Zambia

Malawi

Lubango ●

Mozambique

400 kilometers

400 miles

Namibia

Zimbabwe

Kenya

MAP OF CENTRAL AFRICA

The Sao people lived there from 500 BC through 1500 AD. They didn't leave any written documents so the information we know about them has come from their artifacts of iron, copper, and bronze.

The Kingdom of Zimbabwe was founded around 1200 AD and lasted for 200 years. At the center of the empire was the city of Great Zimbabwe. It was built from huge blocks of granite and some of its ruins still stand today.

GREAT ZIMBABWE RUINS

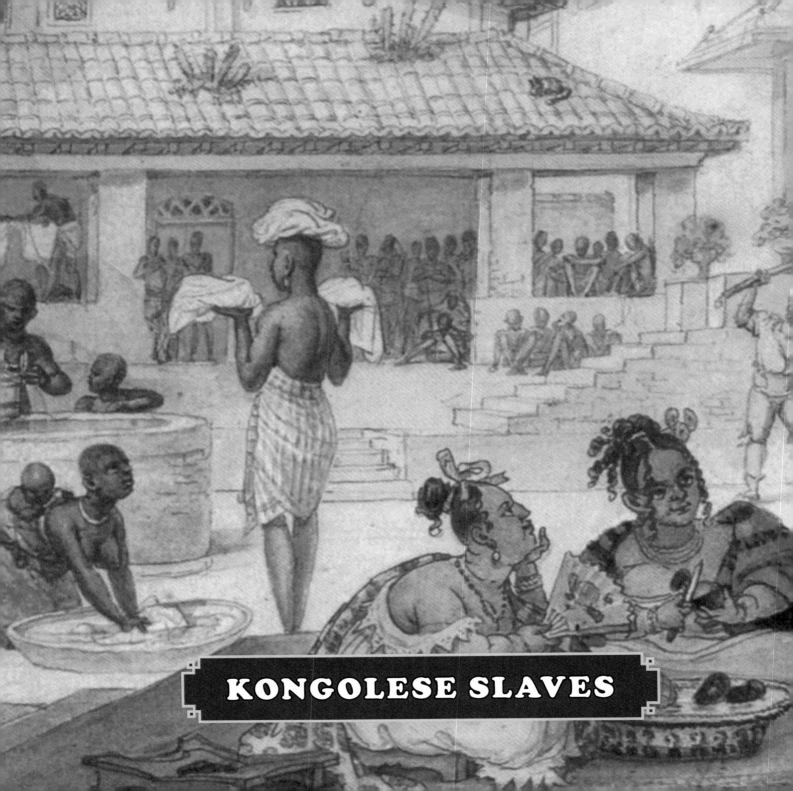

KONGOLESE SLAVES

The Kongo Kingdom rose in power around 1380 AD. It was founded by a great warrior who was called Lukeni lua Nimi. The people used the central African river system to transport goods for export and to carry the imports they had purchased. The Kongolese people were very successful at trading and they grew to a population of over half a million before the Europeans came in 1483 AD.

The Luba Kingdom was founded in 1585 AD. The area where this kingdom was located is now the Democratic Republic of the Congo. Kalala Llunga was considered to be the greatest king during the Luba reign, which lasted more than 300 years. Kalala Llunga's brother Tshibinda founded the kingdom of Lunda in 1665 AD. Both kingdoms expanded until the Europeans arrived toward the later 1800s.

DEMOCRATIC REPUBLIC OF CONGO
COMMUNITY TODAY

The Mutapa Kingdom governed a large section of Africa, which is today the countries of Mozambique and Zimbabwe. A warrior from Zimbabwe founded this kingdom in 1430 AD and it reigned for over 300 years.

ZIMBABWE GONAREZHOU LANDSCAPE
CHILOJO CLIFFS

Awesome! Now you know more about the empires of ancient Africa. You can find more History books from Baby Professor by searching the website of your favorite book retailer.

Visit

BABY PROFESSOR
EDUCATION KIDS

www.BabyProfessorBooks.com

to download Free Baby Professor eBooks
and view our catalog of new and exciting
Children's Books

70378927R00038

Made in the USA
Middletown, DE
13 April 2018